An Invertebrate Fable

Ten sequences of poetry about insects, gastropods and arthropods

Simon Zonenblick

Brambleby Books

An Invertebrate Fable:
Ten sequences of poetry about insects, gastropods and arthropods
Text ©Simon Zonenblick, 2022

All Rights Reserved

No part of this book may be reproduced in any form by photocopying or by any electronic or mechanical means, including information, storage or retrieval systems, without permission in writing from both the copyright owner and the publisher of this book.

ISBN 9781908241696
eISBN 9781908241733

Cover design and layout by Tanya Warren, Creatix

Cover illustration:
Front cover image: two dark green fritillaries resting on orchid bloom, Switzerland, ©Richard Harrington
Back cover images: top: scarce chaser dragonfly (female) ©Adrian Riley
Grove snail, ©Author

Published 2022 by
Brambleby Books Ltd., UK
www.bramblebybooks.co.uk

This book is dedicated to everyone who helps our invertebrate friends in any way.

About the Author

Simon Zonenblick was born in Leeds and has lived in Huddersfield, London, and, since 2012, the Calder Valley, West Yorkshire. He holds horticultural qualifications and has worked as a gardener, in libraries, and in radio and podcasting. His debut publication was *Little Creatures: Poems of Insects, Small Mammals and Micro-organisms* (Caterpillar Poetry 2013) and he has published several pamphlets of poetry and prose. The writer and presenter of a film about Branwell Brontë, Simon also writes nature articles for local papers, along with presenting talks on various subjects.

Fig 1

Foreword

Simon Zonenblick offers a new perspective on the invertebrate world, a world that is easily missed if you don't stop to take a look. A world that contains a horde of tiny creatures that underpin the planet on which we live. In this collection of poems, Simon takes us on a lyrical journey across the vast diversity of the invertebrates that he has observed, presenting each one from his unique personal perspective. The poems are rich with metaphors and imagery, a tumbling, sliding vocabulary that slips, whirs and wriggles into the microcosm, where deep between the grass blades we meet a carnival of exotic creatures. There are poems to delight, some to ponder, and others to wonder at. From dazzling portraits to surreal imaginings, the tone and pace of these verses transform the denizens of the undergrowth into heroes, phantoms and villains, some of which will be left trailing through your thoughts and dreams.

As we drift towards an uncertain future on a raft of crises, poems like these will draw attention to at least one of those problems; that of the many invertebrates that share the world with us. These poems will help readers to appreciate these fascinating creatures in their own right and to admire their discreet charms. An appreciation that will acknowledge the vital roles that these small animals play in maintaining balance in the natural world. Simon's poems amplify the inherent beauty that these invertebrates possess and recognises that beauty leads to a better appreciation which in turn leads to understanding. And understanding is desperately needed at this time of global insect decline.

So read, enjoy and then go into the garden and look. These poems may, like the red admiral in this collection, leave a wisp of their fire etched onto the skyline of your mind.

Peter Smithers, Hon. FRES

Contents

The Caterpillar Chronicles
Elephant hawk-moth 11
Glanville fritillary 12
Sawfly larvae 13

An Oodle of Slugs
Evening scene 15
Ashy-grey slug 16
Netted slug 18
Red slug 19
Dusky slug 20
Leopard slug 21

A Shuffling of Snails
Garden snail shell 23
Roman snail 24
Grove snail 25

Centipedia
House centipede 27
Brown centipede 28
Geophilus carpophagus 29
On a Cornish cliff, I watched you 30

Millipedia
Millipede season 33
The natural history of the millipede 34
Dreaming of millipedes 36
Millipedes of the mind 37

The Beetles
Ground beetle 39
Stag beetle 41

Minotaur	43
Ladybird	44
Weevil	45

An Extravagance of Dragonflies
Dragonfly	47
Dragonfly resting	48
Dragonfly in flight	49

Damselfly Delights
Red damselfly	51
Red damselflies	52
Banded demoiselle	53
Emerald damselflies	54

Lacewing Magic
First sighting	57
Green lacewing	58
Lacewings	59
Lacewing close-up	60
Lacewing wings	61

A Bouquet of Butterflies
Butterfly wings	64
Peacock butterfly	66
Fritillaries	69
Blues	71
Red admiral	72
Orange-tip	75
Butterfly summer	77

Glossary	78
Acknowledgements	82

Fig 2

The Caterpillar Chronicles

Fig 3

Elephant hawk-moth

Blending slug with snake,
snail's pace with feline stealth,
wisps of chiffon, crepe,
with woven smoke,
wobbly eyes bobble as you bodge
through blades of grass
and flatten clovers, stalks
of buttercups or daisies.
Unusual, strange even,
your shuffle ruffles bumblebees
and ants, startles passing bugs and grubs.
Largest of your kind,
grey-squirrel-grey,
you lope a lawn
like the lazy trunk of a languorous elephant
strolling through the jungle.

Glanville fritillary

Velveteen eels,
notch-bodied,
tubular gloops
frazzle-tufted
in quiffs of silver
fluff, your faces
are surprising:
fruit-like, double-domed,
black speck-eyes
upon nuggets of puce;
precisely the same colour
as the feet which dangle
from your hind legs,
like ruby red slippers.

Fig 4

Sawfly larvae

Like lichen-like lizards
you're squiggled stems
of otherworldly plants,
lustrous toadstools
neon streaked,
knobbly wands
of hallucinating wizards,
your bodies
blue, felt-green,
black or white sewn
into tin-foil totem-poles
are tiny plinths of marble,
lathered in marmalade.

Fig 5

Fig 6

An Oodle of Slugs

Evening scene

Slugs, like fat black seals on sea-front snow,
crowd the drizzled concrete,
ebony clouds massing
in a sky of raindrop stars,
bistre blisters,
bronze brigades,
maroon platoons
and coral mobs,
slugs the colour of satsumas
sousing steps and driveways,
announcing saponaceous presences,
kicking back, settling in for the night
and making themselves at home.

Fig 7

Ashy-Grey slug

Like the gooey gearstick
of a car made out of jelly,
a Lilliputian didgeridoo,
a floppy bottle,
viscid cigar,
twisty intestine
stretching to twenty five centimetres!
Lengthiest of slugs,
you furl a curled, pearlescent
blend of blotch and band,
yellowy keel, sludge-back striped black,
cinereally sheathed,
seeking fruits and fungi.

Grand gastropod! You grace
our gardens and illume our woods
in inky glitz, a syrupy surprise
when seen beneath logs
or lounging on beds of leaves and moss,
magnificent mollusk,
splashed like a flag
before an unappreciative world.

Fig 8

Netted slug

Silky slug, shaped
like the lathered lug
of some swamp-slathered,
shuffling squid,
I've seen you taking cover
from the world at walls,
hugging their protective shadows,
reclining on a concrete cushion,
blanketed by leaf mould,
kindred slinker, inching through
a secrecy of grass.

Fig 9

Red slug

Burgundy herbivore,
your orangey-brown body
bulges through the borage,
glinting garnet in cold sunset.

Rufescent round-back!
Rosy rose-gobbler –
rumpled pilgrim,
rubicund wrinkly,
whisky-ish in colour!
Sometimes referred to as the Chocolate Arion,
you're a tentacled North-westerner,
elongating across Europe
like a hunk of russet blubber.

The full extent of your geographical distribution
remains unknown.

Fig 10

Dusky slug

Like a slightly burnt chip
I'll sizzle in the drizzle,

slice my way through continents of cobblestones
slumbering chubbily on dustbin lids,
my blobby body curled
like a sugar-stuffed, slimy smile

and when the time comes I will lay in the evening
in the sunlit grass,
until the night draws in
and the crows are circling.

Fig 11

Leopard slug

Like a strip of elastic liquorice
caramel-carapaced,
glued to the garden wall,
your dark shape
is a breathing statue.
Slithery twist of slimy silk,
you curl, soft-bodied,
in a pirouette of podge,
gauzy gobbler, bingeing
bulge of hunger,
lover of leaves,
you don't know when to stop,
you can't say no,
raid the garden's larder
until you sprawl in a slump
of sun-swollen, smiling slumber.

Fig 12

A Shuffling of Snails

Fig 13

Garden snail shell

Like a hollowed hazelnut
your shell, round-mouthed,
thin-lipped,
is whorled
in spiral bands.

Fig 14

Roman snail

> Your corkscrew shell's a planetary
> crust, a world of whorls
> arched above a stonewash
> hunk, hulked alabaster
> tubed into a body bending
> over stems and stones.

Fig 15

Grove snail

Tongue,
twisty,
silvered cylinder
hooded by a helmet
honed of calcium carbonate.

I've seen you sliding, shyly,
down the undersides of rocks,
camouflaging among rusting leaves
and garden debris,
conical loner,
quiet trudger,
lugging the luggage
of a shelled life
over thorns and stones
and buried bones,
carrying your memories
and hidden treasures.

Fig 16

Fig 17

Centipedia

House centipede

Glassy frazzle, tasseled
lasso of webby legs,
you're a scrabble of scrambling spaghetti,
little limbs tacked
on a wiggling strip.

Unfussy, you'll stake your claim
to outhouses and sheds,
bunk down in compost
or the cool damp secrecy of cellars,
yet you're equally at home in homes,
chancing kitchen tiles,
the humidity of bathrooms,
or trying your luck in the bedrooms of Britain.

Like the elaborate necklace of some fabled Ancient queen,
you stun the viewer with your glistening limbs,
pinnately paired, a century of legs,
symmetrical about your capsule of a trunk,
a shuttling scintilant, seething with venom,
aching to embrace flesh with teeth.

Fig 18

Brown centipede

A slotted slice of segments
wriggling, no longer than the blades
of grass that tuft about you
on all sides,
you're a tube of micro-mottles,
rubbery ringlets fused, twisting,
and the sky's a galaxy away.

Fig 19

Geophilus carpophagus

These glitter-pitted swizzles
jive through soil,
ooze ecru,
writhe in light shows
of nocturnal gold,
tan gritty ground
in citrus streaks,
like veins of sugary blood,
cables sizzling with electric energy,
are eyeless,
blind,
and prefer to be left alone.

Fig 20

On a Cornish cliff, I watched you

On a Cornish cliff, I watched you
propel yourself across a sandy ridge
fringed in the snazzy pizazz of Hottentot figs.

Below us,
craggy scramblings of sand, stone,
rhododendron, roots dug tough
in acid earth
seeped into the sea.

Like a train, you wound a thirty-legged body
over pebble bridges, under tunnels
of seaweed, mossy cuttings,
clambered over stones,
all the while powered by some unseen force
towards a destiny undreamed of
in my philosophies, or yours.

Fig 21

Fig 22

Millipedia

Millipede season

A time of long dark days
and darker nights,
where every body feels softened,
every mouth hungers for detritus,
dead leaves and sweet, decaying delicacy;
every foot feels the urge to scamper,
every waist the urge to twist
and curl in grooving spirals,
every soul the wish to be divided
into distinct sections,
and every eye sees the world in stripes.

Fig 23

The natural history of the millipede

Soil's shuffler,
a lute of spheres,
you sweep,
slug-skinned
but wormy in your habits.

Evolved from watery years
in Silurian seas,
you've been around now
for over four hundred and forty million years!

Crinkled ridge,
your ringleted body's
stem-shaped,
burrows
like a swiveling cigarette,
scoopingly
implodes the troves
of earth's mineral miracles,
aquatic pathways,
as, allured,
you yearn flesh
and blood
and weep for want.

Tell me, wriggling little one,
does your mind sweep back
through Arthropodic centuries
and hold a candle
for your spiracled,
many-legged
forerunners?

Fig 24

Dreaming of millipedes

Like border-seeping oil-slicks,
they spool,
stripy galaxies,
a living,
twisting
jungle of slivery silver,
viperish, leech-like,
slim slugs,
slender devils sliding
like poisoned quills
leaking streaks of Indian ink
across the blackboard of the mind.

Fig 25

Millipedes of the mind

Ringleted re-jiggings of real-life sightings,
now screwdrivering sleet-soft bodies
through the nooks and crannies of the mind,
slick as quicksilver and shimmering
as shiny slime, slipping like streams
down a moonlit mountain
through four hundred million years of evolution.

Fig 26

Fig 27

The
Beetles

Ground beetle

Diversely cosmopolitan,
your family's a gallery of genera.
Crucifix, tiger, bombardier,
zabrus, green raindrops,
agate anti-heroes slicing through the calcium-
coated exoskeletons of insects.
Worm-wolfing, millipede-munching,
carnivorous pills of panther-black poison,
Svelte geckos,
pear-shaped predators who,
like sable-suited robots roam the woods,
you crash your jaws into snail shells,
merciless killer, flesh-impelled;
occasional herbivores,
carrion eaters, diurnal and nocturnal,
colours stretching from metallic black
to golden, dizzy shimmers of peridot-green,
psychedelic opals, tanzanite entrancers,
soapstone psychos, Dick Turpins of the Dust Bowl,
domes of diamantinely-lustred Dichtl lace,
frozen capsules of Coca-Cola,
stylish sports cars, Stone-Age stones.
Away you go, a wriggle of tricks
and sinister secretions,
syndicate of wily pirates,
traversing the continents
and transfixing us with nylon knavery,
you nuggets of black satin,
Triassic tribe, forty thousand strong.

Fig 28

Stag beetle

Curve-crown, you clomp
a soily course through dead
wood, antlered by club-like
hooks.

Like a bully of the undergrowth,
you scuttle, rutting,
horn-headed,
like a moving claw,

purplish matt-black back,
or snowy-speck-sparked tar,
you drag a bruiser's bones,
grislily, a gritty gangster
stamping your authority,
like a warlord brimming
with dictatorial intentions –

and yet, crepuscular Capone,
your food's as far from the carnivorous
as its possible to be:
from larval days of nibbling on decaying wood,
to the sap-sipping habits that define your diet
as a beetle:
confounding expectations,
it's said that through your life
of approximately three to seven years,
you eat nothing whatsoever!

Fig 29

Minotaur

Like an immaculately polished shoe,
you're a bullet of solid gloss,
sheeny shuttle,
black star spinning through space,
elytra grooved like a spinel-spined dybbuk,
crafty assassin, darkling sprite.

Ladybird

Like a blob of lipstick
splodged with mascara,
the ladybird catches light,
pedal-legging over leaves
in twilight rain,
like a small
spray-painted bubble.
Ruby globule,
sliding over stems,
a glutton for greenfly -
this domino-goblin
is a manic ember,
summer's gloss tar-toughening,
hardening this delicate diablo
into a pearly fist.

Fig 30

Weevil

It isn't just your name –
its evil rhyme, which conjures
the sneaky mischief of some hobgoblin
peering from Bosch –
those long, whiskery antennae, too,
drooping from a narrow head
ought, I know, to seem formidable,
should look, I know, like swords
of mercenary knights,
while your bodies of protrusions
should instill instinctive fear.
But somehow, as I glimpse your shadowy shapes
of spiked quicksilver, daggery limbs and mean face
leering in micro-menace,
its affection that I feel.
Danglingly, your feelers hang like wet dreadlocks,
or floppy hats of clumsy magicians,
at times, your elongation veers on the ungainly,
like ambling anteaters, you arch a maudlin crawl,
a trawl through wooden worlds, wary
of the constant threats of spiders, ants, and birds,
and the look of doe-eyed innocence in those stretched
heads, the sadness in your black-blobbed eyes
evokes an empathy that runs so deep
it burns a hole right through all barriers of species.

Fig 31

Fig 32

An Extravagance of Dragonflies

Dragonfly

Quivering blades,
I've seen you slit the mists
above ponds at dawn,
sleek spikes
slice reed fringe,
grassy shallows,
thistled marsh and fen.
Like stained glass naves
your bodies x-ray
spirographs of light;
acid-spangled rainbows
inked
in bleeding
phosphorescences
of layered lace.
Prismatic spires of chemical temples,
like tuxedos of many colours:
vandyl-blue and Greedo-green,
carnelian reds and amaranthine,
maroonly spooling in your spirals
of light,
I've watched you wend
wildflower mysteries
your dancing candle's
arc-of-arrow flames
melting into silvery sapphire,
blending bluely in a blur of sky.

Fig 33

Dragonfly resting

Luminous kazoo
reclining on a bed of grass,
your vitric notes leak
multi-coloured magic
into nitrogen seas.

Your kindled body is a sun-kissed trove
of treasures for the eyes.
Awed, I ache to touch the flame,
refrain
for fear of disturbing this
beautiful surprise.

Dragonfly in flight

Twisting torpedo,
you dip and dive,
like a lightsaber,
draped in crinkled tinsel,
scattering infra-red confetti.
Empyrean laser-beam, aflame,
you lick the humid buzz of summer air,
so all are wakened, and aware
of the jazzy razzle-dazzle of the dragonfly.

Fig 34

Damselfly Delights

Red damselfly

Lazery lace,
you whip
ice-thin wings,
swish in glitzy billows
as you glide, a sliding
shard as shimmery as Tizer,
fizzing in a swivel
of vermilion,
robed in the strobes
of a rose-spun gown.

Red damselflies

Like wands of waterside witches,
they skate a haze of riverside,
scarlet sorcerers
weaving spicy spells
like joss-sticks dipped
in lava, scintillant supernovas,
soaked in sonic gloss.

Fig 35

Banded demoiselle

Weaving through thistles,
your sunlit dance
an elveresque weft,

you float
among saxifrage,
foxtail grass,
fantasias of indigo,
aflame in July's
kisses of soft sunshine.

When skies darken,
and a breeze
clips the tresses of the meadow,
your sliver-thin form sails
like a raindrop on the sea
into hedges tightly knit as cities.

No trace now of your swift
mirage,
a memory of diamonds,
newly chill,
on stone-cold air.

Fig 36

Emerald damselflies

Slivers
of melted malachite,
floating folds of emerald,
silked like quills
of brilliant ink,
verdigris voyagers
dripping in liquefied aventurine,
you drift along the fringes
of the lake at dawn,
striking fragile alchemies.

Fig 37

Lacewing Magic

Fig 38

First sighting

Masked by a fringe of silvery
cow parsley, you lay
like an omen

wings a crystal trick of the light,
clasped to the peeling bark
of a tree upturned
through forgotten toil
or time.

Pearl-pale,
sapphire-spangled,
satin sphinx, sheened
in sunlight, silently
basking in mid-morning peace,
like a sliver of opalescent permafrost.

Fig 39

Green lacewing

Neptunian mermaid,
siren in a sea of thorns,
emerald web,
eyes agog
like two gold globes,
you cruise the woodland's
nooks and crannies,
drifting dart of chlorophyll,
viridescent icicle.

Fig 40

Lacewings

Glaucous swords of elfin villains,
viridian knives of puckish pixies,
you split the petalled curtain
of a woodland stage,
impish insectivores,
dandelion phantoms
serrating sunrise mists
in glittery twists
of turquoise-tinted green,
beryl jesters,
celadon sprites,
luminescent loreleis of aquamarine.

Fig 41

Lacewing close-up

Like a variegated x-ray,
clockwork silhouette,
complex combination of antennae,
twig-bones,
chrysoberyl wings
and blob eyes, gogglesquely globed,
glint-shimmered glider,
minute machine,
helix of the hedgerow,
floating fantasy,
woodland wonder.

Fig 42

Lacewing wings

Like champagne tattoos
they glow silver-snowily,
leaking lustre
on the sunset-flooded skies.

Fragile flakes
of iridescent moonbeam,
rings of Saturn
weeping realms of light.

Fig 43

A Bouquet of Butterflies

Fig 44

Butterfly wings

Illuminated manuscripts,
stained glass windows
of buddleia cathedrals,
nettled nave's cherubim,
tiny harps of woodland minstrels,
petals of dappled alpines,
dripping silver,
gemmiferous fans
of Orient courts,
jonquil-mottled,
billowing bice,
star-slices, iced
and sugared in spice,
diamond-dotted amethysts
twisted into ribbons of gloss,
like roses of the Eastern hills,
cerulean silks,
whispering on breezes
like the secret dreams of spirits
drifting through the margins of known time.

Fig 45

Peacock butterfly

Florid nebula,
your wind-singeing
wings are fuchsia, blue-
blotched in disc-eyes.

Weeping ruby tears tipped in gold,
you imprint yourself on lavender,
fiery flourishes glimmering on gardens
and kindling the breeze.

Fig 46

Fig 47

Fritillaries

Floating flames,
your peachy bodies blur with sunrise,
marigold miscellanies of henna.

I think of you as the fiery flags
of cinnamon planets,
snippets of ginger
waltzing through spring mornings
over marshes and moors,
tripping an auburn saunter
over sunbaked heaths.

Ragwort's ribbons,
you paint tropical pictures
in rockeries, hedge
your bets on betony,
primrose, violets and viburnum,
filipendula, geranium, grasses.
Like the keys of fragile pianos,
you dance over tussocks and herbaceous
borders, pepper woodland verges
in your bronze ballet,
ignite whole swathes of riverside
in ambery fandangos.

Fig 48

Blues

Like fragments of sky,
you're a constellation
of dew-dyed dreams.

Cyan starlets,
fluttering fays,
fairies afloat
in gossamery clouds,
kitschy twinklings,
sprinklings of chintz,
glitzy glissades of sapphire mist.

Your blue beauty
is a fountain of azure,
as flowerbeds tingle
at your luxury touch;
chic chimeras, beryly gems,
cobalt comets,
fleet diadems,
dancing delphiniums,
Favrile sepals,
giggly whirligigs swirlingly pearling
grey noons in festoons
of icing-sugar finery.

Red admiral

Like the momentary vision
of a long-gone love,
you quietly flicker
in a lick of light,
unexpected brilliance,
trickling crimson tickling
lavender, leaves of love-lies-bleeding,
dark as a heart, and soft as newborn skin.

You whisk a dream of forest folklore,
love, and memories
of summers past

and as you float
over the roses
into an onyx sunset,
you leave a wisp of fire
etched onto the skylines of our minds.

Fig 49

Fig 50

Orange-tip

Frosty white flowers,
females jet-edged,
males like sliced snowflakes
dipped in fire,
no mythology
has spoken of your chalky lore
your meadowy ways,

almost unknown in these loud days
of bricks and fumes,
small enough to weave,
unseen, between the borders
of our lands, and lives.

Fig 51

Butterfly summer

Like tiny birds of paradise,
a cosmos of colours,
beaded and banded,
and bleeding in blues,
purples and magentas,
burgundies and emerald,
spectral checkerboards
of silver and gold,
browny blacks, yellows,
velvets and pinks

crystal confetti
of saffron, chalk-white,
tortoiseshells, hairstreaks,
skippers and heath,
ringlets and woods,
topaz trapezists,
jazzy artistes,
kaleidoscopic acrobats,
ballerinas of the blue,
velour heroines
and shamrock mavericks

illuminating meadows,
peppering parks
in momentary sparks,
silken, willowy,
whispers-of-the-wisp,
minute miracles.

Glossary

I have split this glossary into the ten respective parts of the book, with descriptions and information about species featured following the titles, and then with italicized definitions of individual words found in each poem below the poem title concerned. I have restricted these definitions to words pertaining to biology, mythology, or to proper nouns. I have not provided definitions for species of plants featuring in the poems, nor for various types of precious stone and other scientific items used for comparative purposes, except where these are obscure, i.e. I have not defined malachite, but I have defined the mineral spinel, and the chemical compound vandyl.

The Caterpillar Chronicles
Elephant hawk-moth (*Deilephila elpenor*): Up to 80mm; diet mainly willow herbs and bedstraws.
Glanville fritillary (*Melitaea cinxia*): Between 50 and 200 eggs laid on the undersides of ribwort plantain or spiked speedwell.
Sawfly Larvae: 30-90 born in each hatching; often live in colonies.

An Oodle of Slugs
Ashy-grey slug (*Limex cinerioniger*): At longer than 20cm, this is the largest known land slug species in the world. Native to Europe.
Keel: A ridge that runs along the back of some slugs species.
Netted slug (*Deroceras reticulatum*): A milky white slug found in lowland habitats, including gardens. Loves lettuce!
Red slug (*Arion rufus*): One of the "roundback" slugs, *A. rufus* varies from orange to red, to brown and black.
Dusky slug (*Arion fuscus*): Found across North-western Europe, the dusky slug is a 50-70mm roundback.
Leopard slug (*Limax maximus*): A detritivore that consumes dead plants, but is also known to chase and eat other slugs!
Carapace: A protective covering common to a number of animal groups, including arthropods.

A Shuffling of Snails
Garden snail shell (*Cornu aspersum*): The shell of this most common UK snail is heliciform (having the form of a helix / spiral).
Roman snail (*Helix pomatia*): Native across Europe; in Britain the Roman snail lives mainly on chalk soils in the south of England.
Grove snail (*Cepea nemoralis*): Europe-wide, with a vast variety of habitats from coastal dunes to woodlands.

Centipedia
House centipede (*Scutigera coleoptrata*): Up to 15 pairs of legs. Originating in the Mediterranean, now spread almost worldwide. Omnivore, which likes to live in damp environments.
Brown centipede (*Lithobius forficatus*): Europe and beyond. Notable for its dislike of being discovered – the centipede will run for cover very quickly.
***Geophilus carpophagus*:** 51-57 leg pairs; orange to greyish; often marbled appearance.
Ecru: the light beige or fawn colour of unbleached linen or silk.
On a Cornish cliff, I watched you: This poem refers to a sighting, in September 2006, of a small (about half the size of my little finger), brown centipede possessing 30 legs.
Hottentot fig (*Carpobrotus edulis*): A ground creeping plant native to South Africa, which grows in Cornwall and other warm climates. Its common name is inspired by the hairstyles of the Hottentot (Khoikhoi) people of southwestern Africa.

Millipedia
Millipede season: This section covers a generality of millipedes, the Diplopoda, a class of arthropods, one of the oldest groups of animals, originating in the Silurian period, more than four hundred million years ago.
Silurian: Geologic period, spanning 443.8 (+/- 1.5) million years ago to 419.2 (+/- 3.2) million years ago.
Spiracle: external respiratory opening.

The Beetles
Ground beetles: Mostly predatory, taking a large range of invertebrates.
Crucifix, tiger and bombardier, zabrus: Genera of ground beetles.
Dichtyl lace: Type of lace designed in the early twentieth century by the German lace maker, Franziska Dichtl.
Triassic: Geologic period, spanning 251.902 (+/- 0.024) million years ago - 201.3 (+/- 0.2) million years ago.
Stag beetle (*Lucanus cervus*): Named for the male's antler-like jaws, used for courtship rituals and battles with other beetles. Can grow as long as a matchbox.
Capone: American gangster, Alphonse "Al" Capone (1899-1947).
Minotaur: Found on heath and sandy grassland, consumes dung.
Elytra: modified, hardened forewing.
Spinel: A mineral. The minotair beetle's spines are not made of spinel as the poem suggests…
Dybbuk: In Jewish mythology, a dybbuk is the possessing spirit of a deceased person's dislocated soul.
Bosch: Mediaeval Dutch painter, Hieronymus Bosch (*c.* 1450-1516).

An Extravagance of Dragonflies
Vandyl: Vanadyl acetylacetonate, a chemical compound.
Greedo: A Star Wars' villain.
Lightsaber: Star Wars sword.

Damselfly Delights
Large red damselfly (*Pyrrhosoma nymphula*): Prefers small bodies of water and slow-moving rivers.
Banded demoiselle (*Calopteryx splendens,* male): Found across the British Isles, Eastern Europe and as far as Africa and China.
Emerald damselfly (*Lestes sponsa*): A damselfly of ponds, pools and moorland, present in Britain, Central Europe, Asia-Pacific.

Lacewing Magic

Lorelei: According to Wikipedia *'A Rhine mermaid immortalized in the Heinrich Heine poem of that name, [and] has become a synonym for a siren.'* (https://en.wikipedia.org/wiki/Mermaid).

Common green lacewing (*Chrysoperla carnea*): Possibly the commonest UK lacewing, though recent research suggests *C. carnea* may actually represent three different species. These lacewings are unusual in that they hibernate, often in buildings.

A Bouquet of Butterflies

Peacock butterfly (*Aglais io*): The European peacock, also found as far-afield as Asia and Japan.

Fritillaries: Breeding in shaded woodlands, the fritillaries are a well-loved fixture of a British summer, often found on bramble, *Rubus fruticosus*. There is currently much concern over their decline.

Blues: Found on grasslands, heathlands, and gardens – a diverse family which come under the umbrella of Polyommatinae, first listed by the lepidopterist William Swainson in 1827.

Favrile: an iridescent glassware devised by L.C. Tiffany.

Red admiral (*Vanessa atalanta*): Often hosted by stinging nettles, *Urtica dioica, Buddleia, Boehmeria cyllindrica* (false nettles), pellitory, *Parietaria judaica,* and ivy, *Hedera helix,* the red admiral is mainly a visitor to Britain, though increasing numbers seen in their immature stages in the earlier part of the year suggest that they are now resident in some parts of the south of the country.

Orange-tip (*Anthocharis cardamines*): Of the Pieridae family, with body size related to the host plant. Virgin females in flight are always pursued by males, with eventual mating controlled by females.

Acknowledgements

I very much wish to thank the following (as below) for kindly allowing me to use their photographs of invertebrates as displayed in this book. The remaining photos I took myself. I would also like to thank Hugh & Nicola Loxdale of Brambleby Books Ltd. for their unswerving encouragement during the preparation of this book and for their careful editing of the text and help with sourcing and selecting suitable photos to accompany the poems. Lastly, I thank Tanya Warren of Creatix for her superb design and layout of the book.

Photo accreditation: Fig 1: author; Fig. 2: Peacock butterfly larva (*Aglais io*) (DeRebus – Shutterstock.co.uk); Fig. 3: Elephant hawk-moth larva (*Deilephila elpenor*) (Bildagentur Zoonar GmbH – Shutterstock.co.uk); Fig. 4: Glanville fritillary (*Melitaea cinxia*) (Patrick Cook, Butterfly Conservation); Fig. 5: Sawfly larvae (*Arge pagana*) (Anon.); Fig. 6: Black slug (*Arion ater*) (Zonenblick); Fig. 7: Black slug (*Arion ater*) (Zonenblick); Fig. 8: Ash-grey slug (*Limex cinereoniger*) (Zonenblick); Fig. 9: Netted slug (*Deroceras reticulatum*) (fotorauschen – Shutterstock.co.uk); Fig. 10: Red slug (*Arion rufus*) (Zonenblick) Fig. 11: Dusky slug (*Arion subfuscus*) (Josh Mrozowski); Fig. 12: Leopard slug (*Limax maximus*) (Hannah Buckland); Fig. 13: Grove snail (*Cepaea nemoralis*) (Zonenblick); Fig. 14: Garden snails (*Helix aspersa*) (krolya25 – Shutterstock.co.uk); Fig. 15: Roman snail (*Helix pomatia*) (Ian Parker); Fig. 16: Grove snail (*Cepaea nemoralis*) (Steve Byland – Shutterstock.co.uk); Fig. 17: Flat-backed millipede (*Polydesmida* sp.) (Niney Azman – Shutterstock.co.uk); Fig. 18: House centipede (*Scutigera coleoptrata*) (Nigel Partridge); Fig. 19: Brown centipede (*Lithobius forficatus*) (Trevor Pendleton); Fig. 20: *Geophilus carpophagu* (Trevor Pendleton); Fig. 21: Centipede (Zonenblick) Fig. 22: *Pachybolus ligulatus* (Ben Mellan); Fig. 23: White-legged millipede (*Tachypodoiulus niger*) (David Nicholls – naturespot.org.uk); Fig. 24: Thai rainbow millipede (*Tonkinbolus caudulanus*) (Piyapong pc – Shutterstock.co.uk); Fig. 25: Striped millipede

(Portugal) (*Ommatoiulus sabulosus*) (F_N – Shutterstock.co.uk); Fig. 26: Giant African millipede (*Archispirostreptus gigas*) (Millipedes R Us UK); Fig. 27: Ground beetle (Family Carabidae) (Nikolas_profoto – Shutterstock.co.uk); Fig. 28: Stag beetles (male and female) (*Lucanus cervus*) (Kluciar Ivan – Shutterstock.co.uk); Fig, 29: Minotaur beetle (*Typhaeus typhoeus*) (PHOTO FUN – Shutterstock.co.uk); Fig. 30: Ladybird beetle (*Harmonia axyridis*) (Zonenblick); Fig. 31: European acorn weevil (*Curculio glandium*) (Florijn Pockele – Shutterstock.co.uk); Fig. 32: Blue dasher dragonfly (*Pachydiplax longipennis*) (Bonnie Taylor Barry – Shutterstock.co.uk); Fig. 33: Red-veined darter (*Sympetrum fonscolombii*) (Zonenblick); Figs.34: Large red damselfly (*Pyrrhosoma nymphula*) (theedinburghreporter.co.uk); Fig. 35: Large red damselfly (*Pyrrhosoma nymphula*) (David Kitching); Fig. 36: Banded demoiselle (*Calopteryx splendens*) (Ian Parker); Fig. 37: Emerald damselfly (*Lestes sponsa*) (David Kitching); Fig. 38: Green lacewing (Family Chrysopidae) (Marek Mnich –Shutterstock.co.uk); Fig. 39: Green lacewing (Family Chrysopidae) (Lesley Wilson); Fig. 40: Green lacewing (Family Chrysopidae) (Rhonny Dayusasono – Shutterstock.co.uk); Fig. 41: Brown lacewing (Family Hemerobiidae) (Muddy knees –Shutterstock.co.uk); Fig. 42: Close-up of green lacewing (Family Chrysopidae) (InsectWorld – Shutterstock.co.uk); Fig. 43: Green lacewing (Family Chrysopidae) (Cornel Constantin – Shutterstock.co.uk); Figs. 44: Dark green fritillary (*Speyeria aglaja*) (Richard Harrington); Figs. 45: Underside of orange-tip butterfly (male) (*Anthocharis cardamines*) (Richard Harrington); Fig. 46: Peacock butterfly (*Aglais io*) (Richard Harrington); Fig. 47: Dark green fritillary (*Speyeria aglaja*) (Richard Harrington); Fig. 48: Adonis blue butterfly (male) (*Polyommatus bellargus*) (Richard Harrington); Fig. 49: Red admiral butterfly (*Vanessa atalanta*) (Hugh D. Loxdale); Fig.50: Under and upper side of orange-tip butterfly (male) (*Anthocharis cardamines*) (Richard Harrington); Fig. 51: Small tortoiseshell butterfly (*Aglais urticae*) (Zonenblick).

Other Brambleby Poetry Books:

Rings in the Shingle
ISBN 9781908241160

The Butterfly Collection
ISBN 9781908241566

The Worshipful Companies
ISBN 9781908241603

Buzzing!
ISBN 9781908241443

Sirens and Seriemas
ISBN 9781908241368

Flying High
ISBN 9781908241504

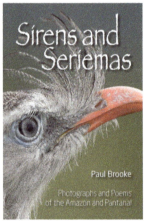

www.bramblebybooks.co.uk

CPSIA information can be obtained
at www.ICGtesting.com
Printed in the USA
BVHW060045180223
658747BV00018B/1726